PRESIDENTS

DWIGHT D. EISENHOWER

A MyReportLinks.com Book

Randy Schultz

MyReportLinks.com Books

an imprint of

 Enslow Publishers, Inc. **E**

Box 398, 40 Industrial Road
Berkeley Heights, NJ 07922
USA

MyReportLinks.com Books, an imprint of Enslow Publishers, Inc. MyReportLinks is a trademark of Enslow Publishers, Inc.

Library of Congress Cataloging-in-Publication Data

Schultz, Randy.
  Dwight D. Eisenhower / Randy Schultz.
      p. cm. — (Presidents)
Summary: A biography of the thirty-fourth president of the United
States, a great general who many believed was too nice to be a great
politician. Includes Internet links to Web sites, source documents, and
photographs related to Dwight David Eisenhower.
Includes bibliographical references and index.
  ISBN 0-7660-5102-1
  1. Eisenhower, Dwight D. (Dwight David), 1890–1969—Juvenile
literature. 2. Presidents—United States—Biography—Juvenile
literature. [1. Eisenhower, Dwight D. (Dwight David), 1890–1969. 2.
Presidents. 3. Generals.] I. Title. II. Series.
E836.S38 2002
973.921'092—dc21

                                        2002015000

Printed in the United States of America

10 9 8 7 6 5 4 3 2 1

To Our Readers:
Through the purchase of this book, you and your library gain access to the Report Links that specifically back up this book.
The Publisher will provide access to the Report Links that back up this book and will keep these Report Links up to date on **www.myreportlinks.com** for three years from the book's first publication date.
We have done our best to make sure all Internet addresses in this book were active and appropriate when we went to press. However, the author and the Publisher have no control over, and assume no liability for, the material available on those Internet sites or on other Web sites they may link to.
The usage of the MyReportLinks.com Books Web site is subject to the terms and conditions stated on the Usage Policy Statement on **www.myreportlinks.com**.
A password may be required to access the Report Links that back up this book. The password is found on the bottom of page 4 of this book.
Any comments or suggestions can be sent by e-mail to comments@myreportlinks.com or to the address on the back cover.

Contents

MyReportLinks.com Books

Great Books, Great Links, Great for Research!

MyReportLinks.com Books present the information you need to learn about your report subject. In addition, they show you where to go on the Internet for more information. The pre-evaluated Report Links that back up this book are kept up to date on **www.myreportlinks.com**. With the purchase of a MyReportLinks.com Books title, you and your library gain access to the Report Links that specifically back up that book. The Report Links save hours of research time and link to dozens—even hundreds—of Web sites, source documents, and photos related to your report topic.

Please see "To Our Readers" on the Copyright page for important information about this book, the MyReportLinks.com Books Web site, and the Report Links that back up this book.

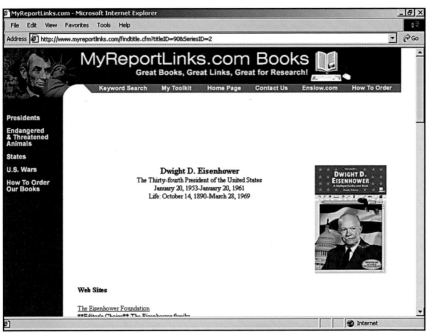

Access:

The Publisher will provide access to the Report Links that back up this book and will try to keep these Report Links up to date on our Web site for three years from the book's first publication date. Please enter **PEI3509** if asked for a password.

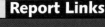 

Report Links

The Internet sites described below can be accessed at
http://www.myreportlinks.com

*EDITOR'S CHOICE

▶ The Eisenhower Foundation
The Eisenhower Foundation Web site provides a family tree, a photo album, and a video clip of Eisenhower during his administration. You will also find biographies of Dwight and Mamie Eisenhower.

Link to this Internet site from http://www.myreportlinks.com

*EDITOR'S CHOICE

▶ Dwight Eisenhower: The Cautious Warrior
Explore Eisenhower's presidency through this comprehensive biography of his life and administration. Here you will learn the details of his life before, during, and after his administration.

Link to this Internet site from http://www.myreportlinks.com

*EDITOR'S CHOICE

▶ The American Experience: Ike
Learn the story of Dwight D. Eisenhower's early career, presidential years, and legacy. You will also find personal correspondences, White House statements, and other resources.

Link to this Internet site from http://www.myreportlinks.com

*EDITOR'S CHOICE

▶ Objects of the Presidency
By navigating through this site you will find objects related to all of the United States presidents, including Dwight D. Eisenhower. You will also find a brief description of Eisenhower and the era he lived in and information about the office of the presidency.

Link to this Internet site from http://www.myreportlinks.com

*EDITOR'S CHOICE

▶ American Presidents:
Life Portraits: Dwight D. Eisenhower
At this Web site you will find "Life Facts" and "Did you Know?" trivia about Dwight D. Eisenhower. You will also find a letter written by Eisenhower to his wife.

Link to this Internet site from http://www.myreportlinks.com

*EDITOR'S CHOICE

▶ Character Above All: Dwight D. Eisenhower Essay
This essay explores the character of Dwight D. Eisenhower. Here you will learn about some of the challenges that Eisenhower faced during his administration and how he handled them.

Link to this Internet site from http://www.myreportlinks.com

 The Internet sites described below can be accessed at
http://www.myreportlinks.com

▶ **The American Experience: D-Day**
Dwight Eisenhower's successful organization of D-Day during the Second
World War led to his promotion to five-star general. At this Web site you
can experience D-Day through images, letters, and news articles.

Link to this Internet site from http://www.myreportlinks.com

▶ **The American Presidency: Dwight D. Eisenhower**
This biography of Dwight D. Eisenhower focuses on his successes in World
War II. You will also learn about his childhood, military career, marriage,
presidency, and retirement.

Link to this Internet site from http://www.myreportlinks.com

▶ **A Brief History of the National Aeronautics
and Space Administration**
This Web site provides a brief history of NASA. Included is Dwight D.
Eisenhower's plan as president to launch a scientific satellite into orbit
around the earth to collect scientific data.

Link to this Internet site from http://www.myreportlinks.com

▶ **Camera on Assignment**
Ollie Atkins was a photographer who worked for the *Saturday Evening Post.*
During Eisenhower's administration, Atkins took many photographs of the
president at work and in social situations. This Web site contains many of
those photographs.

Link to this Internet site from http://www.myreportlinks.com

▶ **Cold War: Dwight David Eisenhower**
At this Web site you will find a profile of Dwight D. Eisenhower. Here you
will learn about his military career and presidency.

Link to this Internet site from http://www.myreportlinks.com

▶ **Dwight D. Eisenhower**
Eisenhower's military career and presidency are profiled in this site.

Link to this Internet site from http://www.myreportlinks.com

Report Links

 The Internet sites described below can be accessed at
http://www.myreportlinks.com

▶ Dwight D. Eisenhower (1890–1969)

At the National Portrait Gallery Web site you will find a painting
of Dwight Eisenhower and a brief summary of his military and
presidential career.

Link to this Internet site from http://www.myreportlinks.com

▶ Dwight D. Eisenhower: "The Fate of the World"

In 1944, Dwight Eisenhower was recognized by *Time Magazine* as Man
of the Year for his strategic planning of D-Day and his effectiveness as a
leader. Here you can read the article written about him.

Link to this Internet site from http://www.myreportlinks.com

▶ The Dwight D. Eisenhower Library and Museum

At the Dwight Eisenhower Library and Museum you can explore
Eisenhower's role in World War II, view historical documents, and
take a virtual tour of the museum.

Link to this Internet site from http://www.myreportlinks.com

▶ Dwight David Eisenhower

At this Web site you will find facts and figures on Dwight D.
Eisenhower, including presidential election results, a list of cabinet
members, notable events, and historical documents.

Link to this Internet site from http://www.myreportlinks.com

▶ Dwight David Eisenhower

The United States Army Web site contains a biography of Dwight
D. Eisenhower. Here you will learn about his life, military career,
and presidency.

Link to this Internet site from http://www.myreportlinks.com

▶ Dwight David Eisenhower: A Leader in War and Peace

At the *New York Times* Web site you can read the obituary of Dwight
D. Eisenhower, who died on March 28, 1969. The obituary highlights
milestones in both Eisenhower's military career and presidency.

Link to this Internet site from http://www.myreportlinks.com

 The Internet sites described below can be accessed at
http://www.myreportlinks.com

▶ **Eisenhower Birthplace State Historical Park**
At Eisenhower's birthplace in Denison, Texas, you explore Eisenhower's poems and painting. You will also find photographs and learn about his legacy and family.

Link to this Internet site from http://www.myreportlinks.com

▶ **Eisenhower Center**
At the Eisenhower Center you will find the biographies of Dwight and Mamie Eisenhower, the Eisenhower family history, and quotations. You will also find facts about D-Day.

Link to this Internet site from http://www.myreportlinks.com

▶ **"I Do Solemnly Swear . . . "**
At this Library of Congress Web site you can experience Dwight D. Eisenhower's first and second inaugurations. You will also find the text of his inaugural addresses and images.

Link to this Internet site from http://www.myreportlinks.com

▶ **The Interstate Highway System**
This Web page explores the history of interstate highways and Dwight D. Eisenhower's role in developing them.

Link to this Internet site from http://www.myreportlinks.com

▶ **Joseph McCarthy**
During Eisenhower's administration, Senator Joseph McCarthy was censured by the Senate. At this Web site you can learn why, while exploring the life and political career of McCarthy.

Link to this Internet site from http://www.myreportlinks.com

▶ **The Life of Dwight D. Eisenhower**
At this Web site you can explore Dwight Eisenhower's military career, presidential career, and read quotes. You can also visit the photo gallery and learn about Eisenhower's top five accomplishments and failures and admired and disliked contemporaries.

Link to this Internet site from http://www.myreportlinks.com

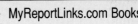
Report Links

▶ **1952 and 1956: Adlai Stevenson (D) vs. Dwight D. Eisenhower (R)**
Here you will find a summary of the 1952 and 1956 presidential elections, the *New York Times* front page coverage of both elections, and an overview of Eisenhower's life.

Link to this Internet site from http://www.myreportlinks.com

▶ **President Dwight D. Eisenhower**
At this Web site you will find a biography of Dwight D. Eisenhower. You will also find an interesting fact about him, a quote, and Eisenhower's first and second inaugural addresses.

Link to this Internet site from http://www.myreportlinks.com

▶ **Speeches by Dwight D. Eisenhower**
This Web site holds the text to four speeches given by Dwight D. Eisenhower.

Link to this Internet site from http://www.myreportlinks.com

▶ ***Sputnik* and the Dawn of the Space Age**
This Web site tells the story of *Sputnik*, the world's first artificial satellite, which was launched on October 4, 1957, by the Soviet Union. It marked the beginning of the space race between the United States and the Soviet Union.

Link to this Internet site from http://www.myreportlinks.com

▶ **The White House: Dwight D. Eisenhower**
The official White House Web site holds the biography of Dwight D. Eisenhower. Here you can learn about Eisenhower's life, military career, and political career.

Link to this Internet site from http://www.myreportlinks.com

▶ **The White House: Mamie Geneva Doud Eisenhower**
The official White House Web site holds the biography of Mamie Geneva Doud Eisenhower. Here you will learn how she met Dwight Eisenhower and about her life as an army wife and First Lady.

Link to this Internet site from http://www.myreportlinks.com

Highlights

1890—*Oct. 14:* Born in Denison, Texas.

1915—*June 12:* Graduates from the United States Military Academy at West Point, New York.

1916—*July 1:* Marries Marie "Mamie" Geneva Doud in Denver, Colorado.

1917—*Sept. 24:* Son, Doud Dwight "Icky" Eisenhower is born.

1918—Serves at Army training post during World War I.

1921—*Jan. 2:* Icky Eisenhower dies.

1922—*Aug. 3:* Son, John Sheldon Doud Eisenhower, is born.

1935–1939—Achieves rank of major and lieutenant colonel; serves as assistant to General Douglas MacArthur in the Philippines.

1942—*June 25:* Is appointed Commanding General, European Theater of Operations.

—*Nov. 8:* Is named commander of Allied forces in North Africa.

1943—*July to Dec.:* Leads Allied invasions of Italy and Sicily.

—*Dec. 24:* Is appointed Supreme Commander of the Allied Expeditionary Force.

1944—*June 6:* Directs the D-Day Invasion, also known as Operation Overlord.

1945—*May 7:* Accepts the surrender of the German army, known as V-E Day.

1948—*June 7:* Is appointed president of Columbia University.

1952—*July:* Receives Republican presidential nomination.

—*Nov. 4:* Is elected thirty-fourth president of the United States.

1953—*July 27:* Armistice is signed ending the Korean War.

1954—*June 17:* Army-McCarthy hearings come to an end.

1956—*Nov. 6:* Is reelected to a second term.

1957—*Sept. 24:* Sends federal troops to Little Rock, Arkansas, to ensure the integration of African-American students in public schools.

1958—NASA (National Aeronautics and Space Administration) is established.

1961—*Jan 20:* Retires to his home in Gettysburg, Pennsylvania.

1969—*March 28:* Dies of heart failure in Washington, D.C.

Chapter 1 ▶

Operation Overlord, 1942

General Dwight D. Eisenhower stood in one of the halls of St. Paul's School, a very famous private school in London, England.

It was May 15, 1944. The world was in the midst of World War II. Eisenhower, the Supreme Commander of the armed forces in Europe, had taken over part of the school for his headquarters.

▶ Eisenhower Appointed

In March 1942, General George C. Marshall had appointed Eisenhower as the head of the Operations Division of the War Department. Eisenhower began plans for an Allied invasion of Europe.

By June 1942, Eisenhower was named commanding general of American forces in the European Theater of Operations. He got the job over 366 senior officers who were eligible for it.

Eisenhower met with President Franklin D. Roosevelt and Prime Minister Winston Churchill of Great Britain to plan the invasion of Europe. They had agreed to cross the English Channel and invade Normandy, in northern France. The plan was called Operation Overlord.

▶ Meeting for D-Day

On this particular day, Eisenhower was meeting with British officials including Churchill, King George VI, British senior staff officers, along with United States

military commanders and senior staff officers. It was to become the largest commanders' conference of World War II, with many of the greatest leaders in military history in attendance. The meeting began at 9:00 A.M.

Those in attendance saw a large relief map of northern France before them. For several minutes, Eisenhower described the plans that had been put together for Operation Overlord, which would eventually be known as the "D-Day Invasion."

Eisenhower concluded his opening remarks by saying, "Here we are, on the eve of a great battle . . . I consider it to be the duty of anyone who sees a flaw in the plan not to hesitate to say so."[1]

On May 17, Eisenhower gave the commanders who had attended the St. Paul's conference the one remaining

▲ *U.S. Army Chief of Staff George C. Marshall (right) appointed Dwight D. Eisenhower (left) to head the Operations Division of the War Department General Staff in March 1942.*

piece of information they needed, the date of the invasion: D-Day would be on Monday, June 5, 1944.

Eisenhower had a personal plan for D-Day—he would watch the amphibious assault land. He might even go ashore once the troops had secured a beachhead, to visit them under fire. When his staff discovered what he had in mind, they were shocked. Suppose Eisenhower got killed?

"Oh that," responded Eisenhower. "Hardly worth worrying about."[2] If there was one thing that Eisenhower took pride in, it was that he paid close attention to the morale of his troops. The general considered good morale to be the greatest single factor for a fighting unit to be successful.

▶ D-Day Arrives

On June 3, just two days before the planned invasion, the weather turned bad. Weather experts predicted that gusty winds blowing across the English Channel would create high waves and make it impossible for landing craft to travel on water. Besides that, clouds had rolled in and rain was falling heavily.

On June 4, weather forecasters predicted calmer weather for the next forty-eight hours. Eisenhower had an important decision to make. He could wait for two weeks until June 19. By then the low tides would once again favor the invasion, but there would be no moon to assist the airborne part of the operation.

Or Eisenhower could order a twenty-four-hour delay and have D-Day on June 6. It was one of the most important decisions of Eisenhower's military leadership. If he sent the first wave of troops across the Channel as planned, bad weather might stop further landings.

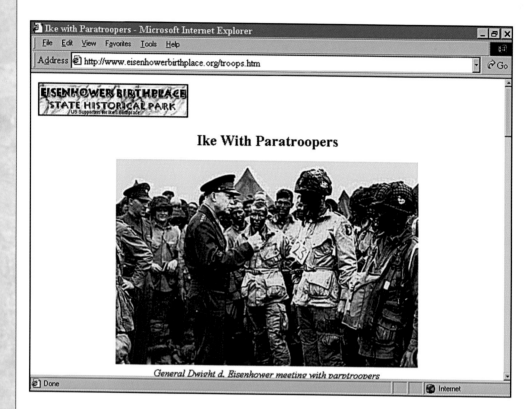

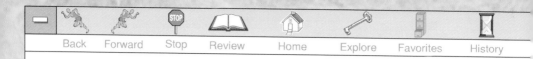

Ike with Paratroopers - Microsoft Internet Explorer

File Edit View Favorites Tools Help

Address http://www.eisenhowerbirthplace.org/troops.htm   Go

EISENHOWER BIRTHPLACE
STATE HISTORICAL PARK
US Supporters for Ike's Birthplace

Ike With Paratroopers

General Dwight d. Eisenhower meeting with paratroopers

Done   Internet

General Eisenhower speaks with paratroopers of the 101st Airbourne at Greenham Common Airfield, in England, before the Normandy Invasion in June 1944.

If he waited two weeks, this heavily guarded secret could leak out and new plans would have to be drawn up.

Eisenhower held a final staff meeting at 4:00 A.M. on June 6. The cloud cover was lifting over the Channel and the heavy rain had slackened.

After weighing every consideration that had been brought to his attention, Eisenhower made his decision.

"Okay, we'll go," commented Eisenhower.[3] D-Day, the greatest amphibious invasion in history (combining land, sea, and air forces), was on.

Chapter 2 ▶

Young Man to Army Man, 1890–1941

Dwight David Eisenhower was born on October 14, 1890, on a rainy night in Denison, Texas. He was the third of seven boys born to David and Ida Eisenhower. The sound of thunder and the pelting rain drowned his cries as he came into the world and the umbilical cord was cut.

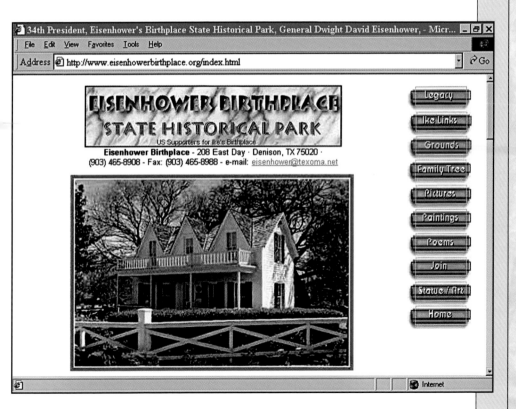

▲ Dwight David Eisenhower was born on October 14, 1890, in Denison, Texas.

Even as his mother cradled her son in her arms, she could not help wondering what might become of him. There had to be something different about a life that began in the middle of a tremendous storm. Ida asked herself, "Wouldn't a child born to lightning flashes and cataclysmic thunder be drawn, as it grew, into a life of violence?"[1]

Although one brother died as an infant, the other five and Dwight grew up together. Dwight's brothers were named Arthur, Edgar, Roy, Earl, and Milton.

The family lived only briefly in Texas. They had gone there following the failure of a general store Dwight's father had managed in Hope, Kansas. Before Dwight was

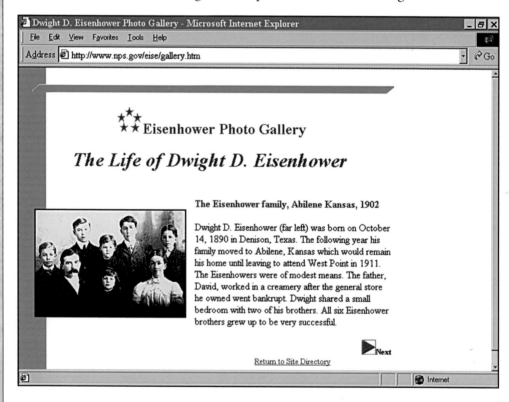

★★ Eisenhower Photo Gallery

The Life of Dwight D. Eisenhower

The Eisenhower family, Abilene Kansas, 1902

Dwight D. Eisenhower (far left) was born on October 14, 1890 in Denison, Texas. The following year his family moved to Abilene, Kansas which would remain his home until leaving to attend West Point in 1911. The Eisenhowers were of modest means. The father, David, worked in a creamery after the general store he owned went bankrupt. Dwight shared a small bedroom with two of his brothers. All six Eisenhower brothers grew up to be very successful.

▶**Next**

Return to Site Directory

▲ *Although of modest means, David and Ida Eisenhower had seven children, all boys. Dwight (far left) was the third child born.*

two, the family had moved back to Kansas and settled in Abilene, where Dwight's father worked in a creamery.

The Eisenhowers struggled to make ends meet. As soon as each Eisenhower son became old enough, he worked in the family garden to help grow vegetables for meals. When they became older they would work odd jobs to raise additional money for the family. As he got older, Dwight worked in the creamery with his father.

The Eisenhower boys grew up in a very religious atmosphere. David and Ida were members of a Protestant church called the River Brethren. Prayer and Bible readings were a daily part of the family's life.

► Grade School

As he was growing up, young Dwight went thorough a life-altering ordeal. He developed blood poisoning in his leg from a scratch. The family doctor advised amputating the young boy's leg, but Dwight protested so strongly, saying he would rather die than lose his leg, that his parents sought other treatments. The leg eventually healed.

In grade school, Edgar was nicknamed Big Ike and Dwight became known as Little Ike. As adults, Little Ike actually stood two inches taller than Big Ike.

Dwight enjoyed school, especially military history. He enjoyed reading about military heroes of the past. When Dwight graduated from high school in 1909, the class yearbook predicted that he would one day become "a professor of history at Yale University."[2]

Unfortunately, Eisenhower's parents could not afford to send him to college following his graduation from high school. For a short time, Dwight Eisenhower took a full-time job at the creamery. His plans were to help pay for brother Edgar's first year of college and then to enter college himself.

▶ Ike Enters the Military

A year after his high school graduation, Eisenhower went to Topeka, Kansas, to take an examination for admittance to the United States Naval Academy in Annapolis, Maryland. When he got there, he found out that an exam was being given for the U.S. Military Academy at West Point, New York.

Eisenhower received the West Point appointment. Because of their religious beliefs, his parents did not approve of his entering the military. As they had done with their other sons, though, the Eisenhowers allowed Dwight to choose his own career.

Eisenhower entered West Point in June 1911. Among his classmates were Omar N. Bradley and James Van Fleet, both of whom would go on, like Eisenhower, to become famous generals.

At one point it was thought that Eisenhower would become a famous football player as a halfback at West Point. Unfortunately, he twisted his knee in a game against the Carlisle Indians and their All-American star, Jim Thorpe. Eisenhower returned for the next game and ended up breaking his knee. Shortly afterward, Eisenhower was forced to give up football. It was a crushing blow, and he even considered leaving the academy.

Eisenhower graduated from West Point in 1915, ranked sixty-first out of a class of 164. The Army then assigned Second Lieutenant Eisenhower to the Nineteenth Infantry at Fort Sam Houston, near San Antonio, Texas.

It was while he was at Fort Sam Houston that Eisenhower met and became engaged to Mamie Geneva Doud, the nineteen-year-old daughter of a wealthy

Denver, Colorado, meatpacker. The Douds spent their winters in San Antonio.

The couple were married on July 1, 1916, the same day that Eisenhower received his promotion to first lieutenant. Dwight and Mamie Eisenhower would have two sons. The first, Doud Dwight "Icky" Eisenhower (born in 1917), died of scarlet fever at the age of three. The second, John Sheldon Doud Eisenhower (born in 1922), eventually graduated from West Point, and became a career army officer like his father.

Sadly, Eisenhower never got over the loss of Icky. Fifty years after the boy's death, Mamie recalled, "It was as if a shining light had gone out in Ike's life. Throughout all the years that followed, the memory of those bleak days was a deep inner pain that never seemed to diminish much."[3]

▲ *Dwight Eisenhower married Mamie Geneva Doud on July 1, 1916.*

▷ World War I and After

As World War I broke out, Eisenhower asked to be sent overseas into combat. The army, though, kept him stationed in the United States as an instructor at various military camps, training tank battalions. In 1918 he served as commander of the tank training center at Camp Colt in Gettysburg, Pennsylvania, and was awarded the Distinguished Service Medal for his work there.

After the end of World War I, Major Eisenhower was assigned to duty as executive director of Camp Gaillard in the Panama Canal Zone from 1922 to 1924. Eisenhower's commander at the time, Brigadier General Fox Connor, was convinced that another world war was on the horizon. Connor convinced Eisenhower to prepare himself to play an important part in that war. With Connor's help, Ike entered the Army General Staff School in Fort Leavenworth, Kansas, in 1925.

Eisenhower worked very hard at the school, graduating first in a class of 275 in 1926. As a result, Eisenhower was chosen two years later to attend the Army War College in Washington, D.C.

◁ *After World War I ended, Lieutenant Colonel Eisenhower was transferred to Camp Meade, Maryland, where he attempted to revolutionize the tactics of tank warfare.*

Major Eisenhower held several posts during the next few years. In 1933, he was appointed an aide to General Douglas MacArthur, then the chief of staff of the U.S. Army. When MacArthur was named military adviser to the Commonwealth of the Philippines in 1935, it was Eisenhower who went with him as his assistant.

In the four years he spent in the Philippines, Eisenhower helped establish the Philippine Air Force and the Philippine Military Academy. Eisenhower even learned how to fly a plane himself.

World War II on the Horizon

Ike returned to the United States in 1939 as an executive officer at Fort Ord, near San Francisco, California. In 1939, as Adolf Hitler's German troops began sweeping through Europe, Eisenhower was certain that the United States would soon be involved in war again.

In March 1941, Eisenhower was promoted to a full colonel. It was just three months later that Ike was made chief of staff of the Third Army with headquarters in San Antonio. He had a brilliant record in large-scale training maneuvers, guiding the Second and Third Armies through military exercises. Eisenhower was promoted to brigadier general in September 1941.

Three months later, the Japanese bombed the U.S. naval base at Pearl Harbor, in Hawaii, and the United States became involved in World War II. Eisenhower, who had been denied action in combat during World War I, was now ready for it.

World War II, 1941–1945

On December 12, 1941, just five days after the Japanese attack on Pearl Harbor, Dwight David Eisenhower received orders from army chief of staff General George Marshall to report for duty with the War Department in Washington, D.C.

It was Eisenhower's job, thanks to his earlier experience in the Philippines, to work on plans to defend the United States possessions in the Pacific Ocean. At the same time, Marshall was beginning his plans for an Allied invasion to fight off the Germans in Europe.

▶ Eisenhower Receives Appointment

In March 1942, Eisenhower was appointed by George Marshall to be the head of the Operations Division of the War

◀ *As Supreme Allied Commander of forces in Europe, Eisenhower was accountable for the strategy, organization, and execution of an Allied victory. However, he was also responsible for keeping the Allied command together. His patience and diplomacy in dealing with military leaders and politicians earned him their respect.*

Department General Staff. Eisenhower was then given the temporary rank of major general.

"Eisenhower, the Department is filled with able men who analyze their problems well but feel compelled always to bring them to me for final solutions," said Marshall. "I must have assistants who will solve their own problems and tell me later what they have done."[1] Marshall hoped Eisenhower would be the type of problem solver that he needed.

Marshall soon found out that Eisenhower was living up to his advance billing. He was the opposite of the kind of officers whom Marshall had no time for: self-seekers, self-publicists, pessimists, buck-passers, the flamboyant, men obsessed with detail. Unlike Eisenhower, Marshall was a loner, but Ike quickly won him over with "affection" and "unlimited admiration and respect."[2]

Eisenhower and his staff developed the plans to unify all American forces in Europe under one commander. They also put together the strategy for opening a "second front" with the invasion of German-occupied France. The first front was Eastern Europe, where the Soviets were trying to fight off the advancing Germans.

In June 1942, just three days after Eisenhower submitted these plans to Marshall, the chief of staff named Eisenhower commanding general of American forces in the European Theater of Operations.

North Africa, Sicily, and Italy

During the summer of 1942, plans were under way for Eisenhower's "Operation Torch," the first major Allied offensive. The lieutenant general met with American and British leaders to plan an invasion of French North Africa and force out the German and Italian armies.

With Eisenhower leading the way as commander of the Allied invasion forces, the Allies landed on the coast of Algeria and Morocco on November 8, 1942. By May 1943 the Allies had taken over North Africa. For his ongoing efforts, Eisenhower was promoted again to full general in February 1943.

With the triumph in North Africa, Eisenhower now turned his full attention to an Allied invasion of Sicily and Italy. Eisenhower had a reputation as an organizer, planner, and a man who could help all of the Allied leaders come to an agreement on their goals and strategy.

By August 17, 1943, the Allies occupied all of Sicily. In September 1943 the Allies invaded Italy. They captured Rome on June 4, 1944, following a long, hard battle.

It was during the Italian campaign that General Eisenhower met with President Franklin D. Roosevelt and Prime Minister Winston Churchill of Great Britain regarding the plans to invade Europe. During this meeting the trio of leaders agreed that the best way to attack Europe would be to cross the English Channel and invade Normandy, in northern France. This plan was called Operation Overlord.

◁ *In Operation Torch, General George S. Patton led the Western Task Force into Morocco during the Allied invasion of North Africa in November 1942.*

In early December 1943, Roosevelt told Eisenhower that he would be in command of Operation Overlord. It was now Eisenhower's responsibility to direct the nearly 3 million troops in the invasion of Europe.

▶ D-Day

At 6:30 A.M. on June 6, 1944, the first wave of troops crossed the choppy English Channel to begin the greatest amphibious invasion in the history of the world.

By nightfall the Allied forces had a firm hold on the beach area of Normandy. But victory in Europe did not come overnight. In fact, it took eleven months of bloody fighting before the Allies claimed victory and freed Europe from German leader Adolf Hitler's control.

"People of the strength and warlike tendencies of the Germans do not give in," said Eisenhower. "They must be beaten to the ground."[3]

On May 7, 1945, Germany finally surrendered to the Allies.

At Eisenhower's French headquarters in Reims, he dictated a message: "The mission of this Allied force was fulfilled at 0241 local time, May 7, 1945." Eisenhower slouched and called for a bottle of champagne in celebration. In London, Churchill declared it was time for the "greatest outburst of joy in the history of mankind."[4]

With victory in Europe, Eisenhower was hailed as America's great hero. In December 1945, President Harry Truman called Eisenhower to Washington, D.C., to name him chief of staff of the U.S. Army, replacing Marshall.

Eisenhower's journey to Washington was just the beginning of his next adventure, one which would make Ike the head of his nation's entire armed forces.

Chapter 4 ▶

Army Chief to President, 1947–1956

In his new role as army chief of staff, General Dwight Eisenhower's largest task was demobilization, or downsizing of the United States Army. Now that the war was over, the United States did not need as many troops on alert. Eisenhower wanted a slow rate of discharge from the armed forces. He also wanted a system of universal military service, which would later evolve into the selective service or the military draft.

Unfortunately for Eisenhower, he had to give in to a peacetime country that was very eager to have its soldiers back home and working again.

So in 1947, Eisenhower worked with President Truman to unify the armed forces under one command. That resulted in the organization of the Department of Defense that would be operated by a single secretary of defense.

▶ Eisenhower Leaves Military

By 1948, Eisenhower felt that he wanted a change. So he retired from active duty to become the president of Columbia University, in New York City. At the same time he wrote a book about his World War II experiences, *Crusade in Europe*. It became an instant best-seller.

Eisenhower was also being sought after by both the Republican and Democratic parties to run for president of the United States. Attempts to have Eisenhower run for president dated all the way back to 1943, during the war. At that time he rejected all offers and he would not even tell what political party he favored.

▲ *Mamie and John watch as Dwight Eisenhower is inaugurated as Columbia University's president in 1948. He served until 1950, when President Truman asked him to serve as the commander of NATO.*

In December 1950, Eisenhower returned to active duty, at the invitation of President Truman, as Supreme Commander of NATO (the North Atlantic Treaty Organization) in Europe. He moved to Europe, taking up his duties at SHAPE (Supreme Headquarters Allied Powers Europe) near Paris, France, in April 1951.

It did not take long for Eisenhower to put together a powerful unified military force. Eisenhower noted that this was the first time that an Allied army had been created to keep peace and not to wage war.

▷ Ike for President

By 1952, Eisenhower was again being sought after to run for president. In January of that year he revealed that he was a member of the Republican Party. Governor Thomas E. Dewey of New York, a Republican presidential candidate in 1944 and 1948, publicly threw his support to Eisenhower.

The Republican Party's endorsement had become too strong for Eisenhower to resist. In June, Eisenhower left Europe and came home to campaign. In July, he retired from the army without pay or military benefits.

In July 1952, at the Republican National Convention in Chicago, Eisenhower was nominated on the first ballot. Senator Richard M. Nixon of California was selected as his vice-presidential running mate. The campaign slogan was "I like Ike."

The Democrats nominated Governor Adlai E. Stevenson of Illinois for president and Senator John J. Sparkman of Alabama for vice president. Near the end of the campaign, Eisenhower promised that he would

▲ Dwight Eisenhower campaigns for president in Baltimore, Maryland, in September 1952.

personally go to Korea to bring an end to the war there. It was a pledge that won him a great deal of support.

Eisenhower was victorious in the presidential election of 1952, capturing 33,936,234 votes to Stevenson's 27,314,992, and with 442 electoral votes to 89.

Even before taking his oath as president, Eisenhower flew to Korea to get a firsthand look at the war. The end of the Korean War would come in the summer, July 27, 1953.

In his inaugural address, Eisenhower covered several areas. In the heart of his address he called for the removal of "the causes of mutual fear and distrust among nations," and he declared that "we must be ready to dare all for our country."

In closing, he said: "The peace we seek, then, is nothing less than the practice and fulfillment of our whole faith . . . More than an escape from death, it is a way of life. More than a haven for the weary, it is a hope for the brave."[1]

When President Eisenhower set about organizing his staff, he based it on what he had learned in the army. For instance, when he named Sherman Adams as assistant to the president, his new title was "chief of staff."

Eisenhower's First Term

In domestic policy, Eisenhower established himself as a "middle of the roader," calling his program "Modern Republicanism." A few weeks after Eisenhower took office, he helped create the Department of Health, Education, and Welfare. The president also approved an expansion of social security and an increase of the national minimum wage to one dollar an hour. Congress also authorized a thirteen-year highway-building program.

Eisenhower also gave the national defense program a "new look." Instead of having a large armed forces, the

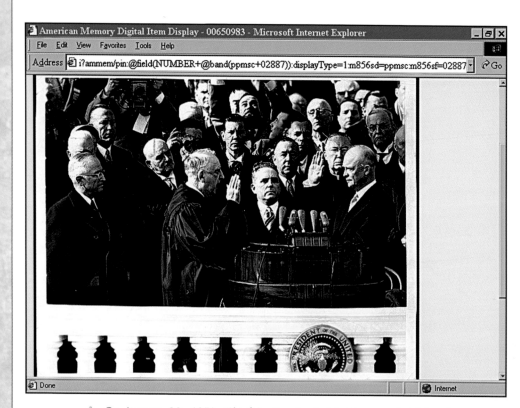

American Memory Digital Item Display - 00650983 - Microsoft Internet Explorer

File Edit View Favorites Tools Help

Address i?ammem/pin:@field(NUMBER+@band(ppmsc+02887)):displayType=1:m856sd=ppmsc:m856sf=02887 ⟳Go

Done   Internet

▲ *On January 20, 1953, Chief Justice Frederick Vinson administered the oath of office to Dwight Eisenhower at the Capitol building, inaugurating him as the nation's thirty-fourth president.*

president made the threat of atomic weapons a main part of the United States' defense policy. Another achievement of the Eisenhower administration was an agreement in 1954 between the United States and Canada to cooperate in building the St. Lawrence Seaway, which by 1959 opened the Great Lakes to ocean-going ships.

The civil rights movement that gained momentum in the 1960s had its beginnings during the Eisenhower administration. In 1954, the Supreme Court, headed by Chief Justice Earl Warren, an Eisenhower appointee, ruled that compulsory segregation in public schools was unconstitutional. Later, Eisenhower sent federal troops to

Arkansas to protect African-American students when a high school in Little Rock was integrated for the first time in 1957.

Just five months after Eisenhower took office, Ethel and Julius Rosenberg were executed as Russian spies. Congress then passed a series of internal security laws in 1954, at Eisenhower's urging. The public's increasing fear of a Communist threat was soon to be fed by a Wisconsin senator.

▶ The Red Scare

In 1953, Senator Joseph R. McCarthy of Wisconsin became the chairman of a Senate subcommittee that began an investigation into Communist infiltration in the government. McCarthy had gained national attention in a 1950 speech in which he accused the State Department of employing Communists and those who sympathized with communism.

McCarthy's tactics involved bullying those he accused, relying on unnamed informants, and not providing credible evidence.

In 1954, the senator turned his attacks on the United States Army as having Communists within its ranks. McCarthy's accusations were then examined in what came to be known as the Army-McCarthy Hearings, and his wild accusations were found to be baseless. His fellow senators voted to censure him, bringing an end to McCarthy's witch-hunts.

Eisenhower was long criticized for not openly denouncing McCarthy, but recent scholarship says that he did work, behind the scenes, to bring about the senator's downfall. The president continued to work at strengthening the United States' alliances with free nations against the spread of communism.

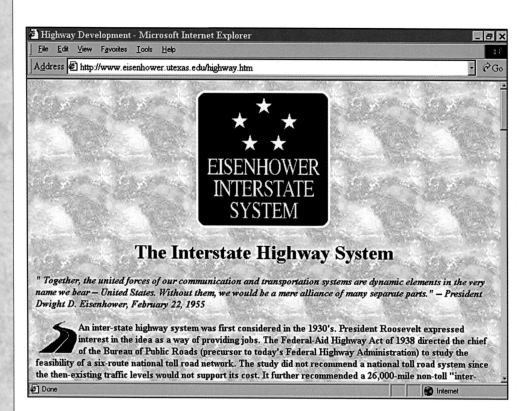

Highway Development - Microsoft Internet Explorer

File   Edit   View   Favorites   Tools   Help

Address http://www.eisenhower.utexas.edu/highway.htm   Go

EISENHOWER INTERSTATE SYSTEM

The Interstate Highway System

" Together, the united forces of our communication and transportation systems are dynamic elements in the very name we bear — United States. Without them, we would be a mere alliance of many separate parts." — President Dwight D. Eisenhower, February 22, 1955

An inter-state highway system was first considered in the 1930's. President Roosevelt expressed interest in the idea as a way of providing jobs. The Federal-Aid Highway Act of 1938 directed the chief of the Bureau of Public Roads (precursor to today's Federal Highway Administration) to study the feasibility of a six-route national toll road network. The study did not recommend a national toll road system since the then-existing traffic levels would not support its cost. It further recommended a 26,000-mile non-toll "inter-

Done   Internet

President Eisenhower is considered one of the fathers of the Interstate system. He pressed for a national highway system after seeing the efficiency of the autobahns in Germany during World War II. Eisenhower signed the Federal-Aid Highway Act of 1956 on June 29 of that year.

In December 1953, Eisenhower proposed that the nations of the world pool atomic information and materials for peaceful purposes. Because of that, sixty-two countries formed the International Atomic Energy Agency in 1957.

Eisenhower and his secretary of state, John Foster Dulles, helped organize eight nations to resist Communist aggression in Southeast Asia. These nations formed the Southeast Asia Treaty Organization (SEATO).

Finally, in July 1955 the leaders from the United States, France, Great Britain, and Russia met in Geneva, Switzerland. Eisenhower made a proposal that the United States and Russia allow air inspection of each other's military bases. The Russians rejected this, as well as other proposals by Western countries.

On September 24, 1955, Eisenhower suffered a heart attack while on vacation in Denver, Colorado. Within three months the president was handling his duties from a hospital suite in Washington, D.C. By December, Eisenhower was back at the White House.

In June 1956 he suffered an inflammation of his small intestine, which required emergency surgery. Nixon presided over cabinet meetings until the president recovered. Although he recovered very quickly, there were many who wondered if Eisenhower's health problems might hurt his chances in running for a second term as president.

A Second Term, 1957–1961

The 1956 presidential election proved to be quite one-sided. Once again, the Republicans nominated Dwight Eisenhower and Richard Nixon. The Democrats once again selected Adlai E. Stevenson as their candidate for president and chose Senator Estes Kefauver of Tennessee as vice president.

During their campaigns, Stevenson accused Eisenhower as being a "part-time" president because of his health problems. He tried telling the American public that Eisenhower might not survive another four-year term.

The president ignored such threats, instead telling Americans that he would give them four more years of "peace and prosperity."

Eisenhower and Nixon won the election by an even bigger landslide victory than they had in 1952. Eisenhower received 35,590,474 popular votes to 26,022,752 for Stevenson, as well as 457 electoral votes to 73. Eisenhower and Nixon were the first Republican president and vice president to be reelected as a team. Unfortunately for Ike, he became the first president in more than a hundred years without a majority of his party in either the Senate or House of Representatives.

▶ Eisenhower's Second Term

Stevenson's words regarding Eisenhower's health echoed in many Americans' ears when Ike suffered a mild stroke on November 25, 1957. The stroke affected his speech for a short time, but Eisenhower regained his complete health soon enough.

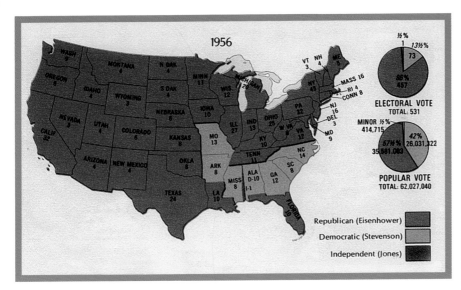

1956

½ %
1   13½%
73
86%
457

VT NH ME
3   4   5
MASS 16
RI 4
CONN 8

ELECTORAL VOTE
TOTAL: 531

MINOR ½%
414,715

42%
26,031,322
57½%
35,581,003

POPULAR VOTE
TOTAL: 62,027,040

Republican (Eisenhower)
Democratic (Stevenson)
Independent (Jones)

▲ Map of the presidential election of 1956.

On October 4, 1957, the "Space Age" began when Russia startled the world by launching *Sputnik,* the first man-made space satellite. The American public was stunned by the event and began wondering how far behind their country could be in the space race. Eisenhower immediately set up the office of Special Assistant to the President for Science and Technology to advise him.

America answered the question when it launched *Explorer I* on January 31, 1958. In July of that year, Congress established the National Aeronautics and Space Administration (NASA) to oversee America's efforts in space exploration.

There were other problems for the Eisenhower administration to deal with at home. The economy took a downturn in 1957 and 1958. The president was against a broad government spending program, believing that

it would lead to inflation. The economy rallied by the summer of 1958.

Congressional elections in 1958 led to even more Democratic victories. Eisenhower became the first president to serve with three Congresses controlled by the opposing party. Getting support for his programs became extremely difficult.

▶ Foreign Affairs

It was just a year before that Congress had approved, at the request of Eisenhower, a new foreign-policy posture which came to be known as the "Eisenhower Doctrine." This authorized the president to use armed force to aid any nation or group of nations that wanted to fight communism. When the government of Lebanon requested such assistance in 1958, Eisenhower sent the U.S. Marines to protect that small Middle Eastern country.[1]

There was aid being offered to China. Communist China threatened to invade Formosa (later called Taiwan) in September 1958 and began shelling islands between Formosa and the Chinese mainland. The president ordered the U.S. Navy to provide protection for Chinese nationalist ships supplying military outposts on the islands. By October the Communists' attacks had died down.

Eisenhower hoped to ease the tensions between the United States and the Soviet Union. Eisenhower entertained Soviet Premier Nikita S. Khrushchev in September 1959. Things seemed to be going well between them as they conducted their conference. A second summit conference and a return visit by Eisenhower to Russia was planned for Paris, France, in 1960.

Those plans were dashed in May 1960 when the Soviets shot down an American U-2 reconnaissance plane piloted by Francis Gary Powers over Soviet territory. Eisenhower admitted that "spy" flights over the Soviet Union had been going on for four years.[2]

Khrushchev demanded that Eisenhower personally apologize for the spy flights. When the President refused, the Soviet premier withdrew the invitation for Eisenhower to visit Moscow. A Soviet court convicted Powers of espionage, but he was released in 1962 in an exchange for a Soviet spy.

The final foreign-affairs chapter in Eisenhower's administration began in 1959 when Fidel Castro seized power in Cuba. Castro adopted a violent anti-American policy. By 1960, Castro seized all property owned by American companies in Cuba. Castro later charged that the United States embassy in Havana was the center of "counter-revolutionary activities" against Cuba.

On January 3, 1961, just days before the end of his term as president, Eisenhower broke off all diplomatic relations with Cuba.

Despite Eisenhower's support of ▷ Vice President Nixon, Senator John F. Kennedy of Massachusetts won the presidential election of 1960. However, Nixon would go on to win the presidential race of 1968.

▷ Ike's Final Presidential Days

Eisenhower was the first president to be prevented from running for a third term by the Twenty-second Amendment. The amendment had become law in 1951 and limited a president to two full elected terms.

During the campaign for the 1960 elections, Eisenhower threw his support to Vice President Nixon, who had been nominated by the Republican Party. Nixon narrowly lost the presidency to Senator John F. Kennedy of Massachusetts.

When Eisenhower left office at age seventy, the oldest man ever to be president to that period of time, he delivered a farewell address on January 17, 1961.

> To all the peoples of the world, I once more give expression to America's prayerful and continuing aspiration . . . We pray that peoples of all faiths, all races, all nations may have their great human needs satisfied; that those now denied opportunity shall come to enjoy it to the full; that all who yearn for freedom will understand, also, its heavy responsibilities; that all who are insensitive to the needs of others will learn charity; that the scourges of poverty, disease, and ignorance will be made to disappear from the earth, and that, in the goodness of time, all peoples will come to live together in a peace guaranteed by the binding force of mutual respect and love . . . [3]

Chapter 6

His Days After Office, 1961–1969

The day before John F. Kennedy took office, Eisenhower met with him one last time, this time in the president's Oval Office in the White House. Alone, the two men discussed several matters. One was having Eisenhower show Kennedy how to use the code book and the prototypical laptop computer contained in a satchel.

▶ The Secret Codes

Better known as "the Football," the satchel was never far from the president. With a special presidential identity card placed into the computer, the president could then look up the special codes needed to launch a nuclear attack and punch them in.

From the Oval Office, Eisenhower and Kennedy stepped into the Cabinet room. The main subject of their discussion was Laos, an neighbor of Vietnam. Eisenhower felt that if Laos fell to the Communists, it was only a matter of time before South Vietnam, Cambodia, Thailand, and Burma would fall, too.[1]

On December 6, 1960, President ▶ Eisenhower welcomed President-elect John F. Kennedy to the White House.

On January 20, 1961, Kennedy was sworn in as the country's thirty-fifth president. Like many other Americans listening to Kennedy, Eisenhower heard the new commander-in-chief say, "The torch has been passed to a new generation . . ."[2]

▶ Eisenhower the Civilian

The next day, Eisenhower was back to living a civilian's life. He retired to his farm near Gettysburg, Pennsylvania. There he wrote two volumes of memoirs of his two terms as president. The first was titled *Mandate for Change;* the second volume was called *Waging Peace.*

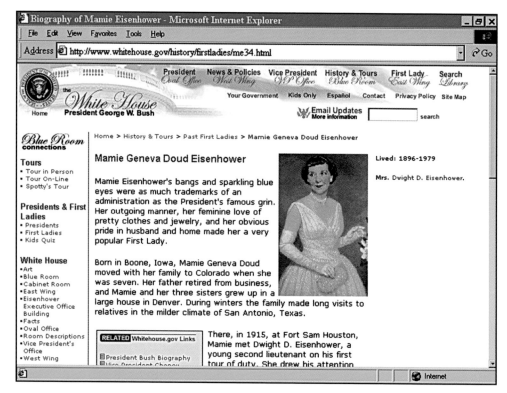

▲ *Mamie Eisenhower was a popular First Lady.*

Mamie Eisenhower had done everything a wife could do to turn the Gettysburg farmhouse into a real home for them. She had started remodeling the home back in 1955. By 1958 the remodeling was complete and the house was ready to be lived in.

Actually, the Eisenhowers did not live at Gettysburg all the time. In the winter, Eisenhower preferred the warmth and comfort of their house at the El Mirador Country Club in Palm Springs, California.

Two months after Eisenhower left the presidency, Congress restored his rank as General of the Army. Eisenhower was entitled to receive a pension for being a retired president so he did not receive a general's salary.

Ike's Accomplishments

Dwight D. Eisenhower was proud of his administrations' accomplishments from 1953 to 1961. In a memo written by him in 1965, Eisenhower pointed out those accomplishments, including:

- Statehood for Alaska and Hawaii
- Building of the St. Lawrence Seaway
- End of the Korean War; hereafter no American killed in combat
- Largest reduction in federal taxes to that time
- First Civil Rights law in eighty years
- Prevention of Communistic efforts to dominate Iran, Guatemala, Lebanon, Formosa (Taiwan), South Vietnam
- Reorganization of the Defense Department
- Initiation, and great progress in, most ambitious road program by any nation in all history
- Slowing up and practical elimination of inflation
- Initiation of Space program with successful orbit in less than three years

- Initiating a strong ballistic missile program
- Conceiving and building the Polaris program of underwater missiles
- Starting federal medical care for the aged
- Desegregation in Washington, D.C.
- Defense Education Bill
- Using Federal power to enforce orders of a federal court in Arkansas, with no loss of life
- Establishment of the Department of Health, Education, and Welfare
- Initiating of plan for social program in Latin America (later called Alliance for Progress)
- Atoms for Peace proposal in which the United Nations would collect nuclear materials, and try to find peaceful uses for nuclear energy.

All of this was done with a Congress controlled by the opposition party for six years. Eisenhower's greatest satisfaction, though, was not his presidency. It was his years as Supreme Allied Commander in World War II. The wartime adventures and comradeships were larger, and meant more, with age. "As the years go by I think that today I feel closer to the individuals of the Allied Forces of World War II than even when we were all together," Eisenhower said.[3]

▶ Final Years

In March 1968, Eisenhower suffered his third heart attack. He was flown to Walter Reed Hospital in Washington, D.C., from California. Eisenhower suffered his fourth heart attack in August. Although he survived again, this time a large pacemaker was placed inside his chest.

On March 28, 1969, Dwight D. Eisenhower died of congestive heart failure at the age of seventy-eight at

Walter Reed Hospital. Eisenhower was buried at his boyhood home in Abilene, Kansas.

Toward the end of his life, Eisenhower had expressed great satisfaction with his presidency, but also voiced his greatest disappointment.

"One of my major regrets is that as we left the White House I had to admit to little success in making progress in global disarmament or in reducing the bitterness of the East-West struggle," said Eisenhower. "But though, in this, I suffered my greatest disappointment, it has not destroyed my faith that in the next generation, the next century, the next millennium these things will come to pass."[4]

During the last eight years of Dwight Eisenhower's life, Americans no longer seemed to consider him the commanding leader they had elected by the landslides of 1952 and 1956. According to the Gallup Poll, people still admired him more than almost anyone else in the country (from 1946 to 1969, he was consistently first or second on this list, except for 1964, when he was third).

Politically, though, they no longer seemed to take him seriously. As David Eisenhower, Ike's grandson, lamented in a 1968 letter to Richard Nixon, "My Granddad is now regarded as a simple country bumpkin and a sweet old General."[5]

Dwight D. Eisenhower will be ▶ *forever remembered as ". . . too nice a person to be a politician."*

In March 1969, a *New York Times* reporter who went to Times Square to conduct street interviews after Eisenhower's death heard these remarks: "He was a great soldier . . . As a President, he did the best he knew how. . . . He wasn't the greatest American President but everywhere he went, he improved our image in the world. . . . He was too nice a person to be a politician."[6]

Today there are several memorials that pay tribute to Eisenhower's life. In Abilene, Kansas, the original Eisenhower homestead is on display. Also located there is the Eisenhower Presidential Library and a chapel that Eisenhower helped design. He and his wife are buried there, along with their infant son.

Eisenhower's home in Gettysburg, Pennsylvania, is also a national historic site and memorial to the former president. Buried inside one of the brick chimneys of the farmhouse at Gettysburg is a copper box that Eisenhower quietly installed while president, telling almost no one. Sealed inside the copper box, alongside artifacts of his life and work, are two documents.

The few who know much about them believe the first document to be his no-holds-barred assessment of the Allied officers who served under him in World War II. The second is said to be a message to future Americans about the politics of the United States and the world.

Under Eisenhower's precise wishes, his time capsule with those documents will not be opened until well into the twenty-first century. Whatever future historians write of his career, the Supreme Allied Commander and thirty-fourth president of the United States has ensured that he will have at least the next-to-last word.[7]

Chapter Notes

Chapter 1. Operation Overlord, 1942

1. Michael R. Beschloss, *Eisenhower: A Centennial Life* (New York: HarperCollins Publishers, 1990), p. 274.

2. Ibid., p. 276.

3. Ibid., p. 281.

Chapter 2. Young Man to Army Man, 1890–1941

1. Merle Miller, *Ike the Soldier* (New York: Crown Publishing Group, 1985), p. 59.

2. David C. Whitney, *The American Presidents* (Garden City, N.Y.: Doubleday & Company, 1985), p. 293.

3. Michael R. Beschloss, *Eisenhower: A Centennial Life* (New York: HarperCollins Publishers, 1990), p. 28.

Chapter 3. World War II, 1941–1945

1. George C. Marshall, as posted by *eHistory.com*, "Marshall's Protégé," eHistory.com, n.d., <http://www.ehistory.com/world/library/books/wwii/army/ike/0006.cfm> (March 14, 2003).

2. Michael R. Beschloss, *Eisenhower: A Centennial Life* (New York: HarperCollins Publishers, 1990), p. 38.

3. Ibid., p. 69.

4. Paul H. Liben, "The Ever-Relevant Message," *Winston Churchill—Fulton*, 1989, <http://www.winstonchurchill.org/wliben.htm> (March 14, 2003).

Chapter 4. Army Chief to President, 1947–1956

1. Dwight D. Eisenhower, "First Inaugural Address," *Inaugural Addresses of the Presidents of the United States*, 1989, <http://www.bartleby.com/124/pres54.html> (March 14, 2003).

Chapter 5. A Second Term, 1957–1961

1. Dwight D. Eisenhower, "Special Message to the Congress on the Situation in the Middle East," *The Dwight D. Eisenhower Library*, January 5, 1957, <http://www.eisenhower.utexas.edu/midleast.htm> (March 14, 2003).

2. David C. Whitney, *The American Presidents* (New York: Doubleday & Company, Inc., 1985), p. 299.

3. Dwight D. Eisenhower, "Farewell Address," *The Dwight D. Eisenhower Library,* January 17, 1961, <http://www.eisenhower.utexas.edu/farewell.htm> (March 14, 2003).

Chapter 6. His Days After Office, 1961–1969

1. Michael R. Beschloss, *Eisenhower: A Centennial Life* (New York: HarperCollins Publishers, 1990), p. 600.

2. John F. Kennedy, "Inaugural Address of John F. Kennedy," *The Avalon Project at Yale Law School,* January 20, 1961, <http://www.yale.edu/lawweb/avalon/presiden/inaug/kennedy.htm> (March 14, 2003).

3. Beschloss, p. 606.

4. Dwight D. Eisenhower, "Ike," *The American Experience: The Presidents,* 1997, <http://www.pbs.org/wgbh/amex/presidents/nf/teach/eisen/eiseniq.html> (March 14, 2003).

5. Beschloss, p. 215.

6. Ibid.

7. Ibid., p. 228.

Further Reading

Ambrose, Stephen E. *The Good Fight: How World War II Was Won.* New York: Atheneum Books for Young Readers, 2001.

Brenner, Samuel. *Dwight D. Eisenhower.* San Diego, Calif.: Greenhaven Press, Inc., 2002.

Brown, D. Clayton, *Dwight D. Eisenhower.* Springfield, N.J.: Enslow Publishers, Inc., 1998.

Cannon, Marion G. *Dwight David Eisenhower: War Hero and President.* Danbury, Conn.: Franklin Watts, 1990.

Darby, Jean. *Dwight D. Eisenhower: A Man Called Ike.* Minneapolis: Lerner Publishing Group, 1990.

Hatt, Christine. *World War II, 1939–45.* Danbury, Conn.: Franklin Watts, 2001.

Hudson, Wilma J. *Dwight D. Eisenhower: Young Military Leader.* New York: Aladdin Paperbacks, 1992.

Joseph, Paul. *Dwight D. Eisenhower.* Minneapolis: ABDO Publishing Company, 1998.

Lindop, Edmund. *Dwight D. Eisenhower, John F. Kennedy, Lyndon B. Johnson.* Brookfield, Conn.: Twenty-First Century Books, 1996.

Lucas, Eileen. *Eisenhower, Kennedy, and Johnson.* Vero Beach, Fla.: Rourke Corporation, 1996.

Speakman, Jay. *The Cold War.* Farmington Hills, Mich.: Gale Group, 2001.